April in Paris

A comedy

John Godber

D1638135

Samuel French — London
New York - Toronto - Hollywood

APRIL IN PARIS

First performed on 23 April 1992 at the Spring Street
Theatre, Hull, by the Hull Truck Theatre Company as
part of the Hull 1992 Festival.

Al	John Godber
Bet	Jane Clifford

Directed by John Godber
Designed by Rob Jones
Director's Assistant Zoe Seaton

The action takes place in a space representing several
locations

Time — the present

To Jane

Other Plays by John Godber published by
Samuel French Ltd

Happy Families
Salt of the Earth
Teechers
Up 'n' Under

ACT I

Playover: Edith Piaf Collection

A space. In the middle of the space is a white box (a white floor and white flats about 10 feet square). Two white chairs fill the box. A hanging light (practical) is visible

Introduction music plays, a laconic French tune. The House Lights fade. Bet enters. She is wearing black and white. She sits on a chair and reads a copy of Bella *magazine*

The Lights fade. Al enters. He is a large, distraught man in his late thirties, also wearing black and white. Music fades

Al Are you back?
Bet No.
Al Oh.
Bet Yeah.
Al Oh.
Bet Yeah.
Al Do you want a coffcc making?
Bet No.
Al Are you sure?
Bet Yeah.
Al Oh.
Bet ˙Been int shed?
Al Yeah.
Bet Oh ...
Al All day ...
Bet Ah ...
Al Yeah.
Bet How's it going?
Al All rate.
Bet Nowt ont telly.
Al No.

Bet Cold in here.
Al Heating's on.
Bet Is it?
Al Yeh.
Bet (*looking at the magazine*) Oh, this looks good.
Al Shall I make a pot of tea?
Bet I'm not bothered.
Al I'll leave it then.
Bet (*looking at the magazine*) Oh yes, this looks good.
Al What is it?
Bet A competition.
Al Oh.
Bet Well ...
Al Don't enter another competition.
Bet Why not?
Al It's embarrassing.
Bet It is not.
Al What are you trying to win?
Bet A life.
Al A life ...
Bet Somewhere away from you ...
Al Oh ...
Bet Somewhere nice ...
Al I'll help you do it if you want.
Bet You've no need.
Al What do you win?
Bet I'm not telling you.
Al It's full of rubbish anyway ...

Silence. Bet sits and reads Bella

Bet (*reading the magazine*) Oh this is interesting. It says here that according to a survey most Yorkshire men would prefer a pint than making love with their wives.

Pause

Al What sort of pint?
Bet It says twenty per cent would rather go to the pub.

Al If they've got any money.

Bet And that fifty-one per cent would rather pursue a hobby, that's you. Oh, they watch twenty-one hours telly a week — I wonder if that includes videos — and listen to twelve hours music, well, that's not you — you hate music, don't you?

Al At least I don't read rubbish.

Bet It's not rubbish.

Al At least I read sommat decent.

Bet 'S boring what you read. Just a load of pictures.

Pause

Al Many in town?

Bet Empty.

Al No money about.

Bet I tret myself to a little treat today. Sommat to wear.

Al What was it, a gas mask?

Bet You think you're funny.

Al I did once.

Bet A scarf. There's nobody shopping in town. There's tumbleweed blowing around the streets.

Al Better tell the Council, they should see to that.

Bet Bought myself a scarf. Saved up, made me feel a bit better, cheered me up a bit.

Al You should've got me one. I suit a scarf.

Bet Oh you.

Al What?

Bet You think you're so funny.

Silence. Bet sees something in the magazine

Bet Hey, I think I can do this one.

Al You say that about them all.

Bet I know this one.

Al Don't enter another competition for God's sake.

Bet Shut up you.

Al It's all a fix. You've got more chance of flying to the moon.

Bet Don't be such a spoilsport.

Al You never win owt.

Bet I nearly won a Jaguar once. I only entered that for you. That thing in
  the supermarket, win a Jag, I entered that one for you.
Al You entered for yourself.
Bet I can't drive.

Silence

Al You never win owt.
Bet I won a cool bag ... four golf balls ... I won some dog food once ...
Al How's it going at work?
Bet All rate ...
Al Ohhhhhh.

Silence

Bet Is it finished? That thing you're doing?
Al It's not a thing I'm doing.
Bet Go and get it, let's have a look.
Al No. You're not interested.
Bet Go on. Go on, let's have a look at it, it might be a masterpiece.

  Al gets up and slowly exits

  (*Calling off after him*) Go and bring it for me. Because if I don't see it
  you'll only have a tantrum and hit a door ... or sommat ...

  *Al enters carrying a large canvas with an awful, monochromatic
  amateur painting of an industrial landscape on it. He is shy but proud*

Al I can hear you by the way, walls are paper thin.
Bet I haven't said owt.
Al Here you are.
Bet (*overreacting*) Oh, oh, that's good, int it?
Al Not bad is it?
Bet It's like your others.
Al I know. I try and paint sommat different but it always turns out like this.
Bet And all them books you read about painting and all? No, it's good.
  It's great.
Al It's not quite finished yet. I've got to sign it.

Bet It looks finished to me. Completely finished.
Al Don't be so funny.
Bet Do you know it's lovely is that, and it'll come in handy.
Al Can we hang it in the house?
Bet It can go upstairs and stop that draught in the loo.
Al Shall I take it back?
Bet If you want, don't ask me everything.
Al I'll take it back, then, shall I?

He exits

Bet (*calling after him*) Rita at work asked if we wanted to go out with them. Her and Colin are going to that Over Twenty-Fives' Night in town.

Al enters

She says it's a great laugh. She's asked me if we want to go. I said I'd ask you.
Al What should I want to go for?
Bet For a laugh, be all right, you'll get in, you're old enough.
Al I'm not going, no point to it.
Bet There is for a laugh, look on the bright side.
Al There isn't a bright side. We've got six thousand to live on, now we can either pay the house off or be buried, take your pick.
Bet Oh, don't start.
Al And you're wanting to go to discos.
Bet Well, you never do owt.
Al Twenty years with that firm, building bloody boxes like this for people to sodding live in. A good wind would blow 'em over.
Bet They're nice houses.
Al Sat about in the back garden with the shirt off, showing off. And housewives bringing you tea and biscuits, treating you like gods. A god in their back garden. And they'd look at you and you'd know what they were thinking ...
Bet Well, I bet they weren't thinking it about you.
Al I feel like a bloody leper now, I'm dropping to bits.
Bet I wish you were still at work, I do.
Al And kids nicking stuff off the site every night.

Bet At least I didn't see that much of you ...

Al Why? And then we'd build 'em and the next thing you know they're covered in graffiti.

Bet I'd forgotten what it was like spending nearly every waking hour with you.

Al First four months, I thought it was great. No need to get up in a morning. Stay in bed all day, all night. And then it starts to get to you ... You get up, light a fire, walk to the gate, come back, look at the fire. Go back to bed, might as well be dead.

Bet I wish you were sometimes.

Al I thought it would soon be over, but I was bloody wrong.

Bet Go in the shed if you're going to shout.

Al Sat in here all day ...

Bet I wish I could get my hands on whoever shut that firm. I'd bloody shoot 'em.

Al This bloody house.

Bet Just leave it.

Al Where's the money going to come from? Every penny you get you spend.

Bet That's not true.

Al Bloody records, scarves, God knows what else.

Bet I haven't bought any records for years.

Al Bloody scarves.

Bet It cost me four pounds, that's all.

Al I'm redundant living in a bloody shed and you're swanning about buying scarves. Who do you think you are, Princess Anne?

Bet I have a right to tret myself.

Al You're buying scarves and we can't even go out for a drink.

Bet You don't want to go out. We could go out and have a drink with Rita and Colin if you like. But you're too miserable, we could go out with them and have one drink.

Al I'm not just having one drink. You go out with them if you want, but I'm not going out and sitting there all night with one drink.

Bet No, I should've known. One drink's no good for you, is it?

Al No, it's not.

Bet You've got to have eight.

Al You think you're funny. I could kill you sometimes, you right get under my skin.

Bet And I could kill you and all, I could slit your throat and think I'd done nowt.

Al Go on do it then.

Bet I'll smash every painting in that bloody shed if you start.

Al Go on then.

Bet I could do better myself.

Al Could you?

Bet I could do better than you.

Al Could you?

Bet I could.

Al You couldn't.

Bet What do you do 'em for anyway, you won't let anybody see 'em, mind you, there's no wonder, I'd be ashamed.

Al I do 'em for me. For me. Not for you, for me.

Bet Yeah, typical, all for yourself.

Al Shut up you and go and enter another competition. Hey, look at the time, it's ten to eight. You haven't entered a competition for an hour. Are you ill or sommat? I'll ring a doctor, shall I? It might be withdrawal symptoms. Hey I tell you what, I've seen one tonight. There's one in the paper, win a muzzle. Why don't you enter that?

Bet You want a muzzle.

Al Do I?

Bet You do.

Al I think I'll start entering, see if I can win a job.

Bet Oh was that a joke? That's not like you to make a joke.

Al It's the only way I'm gonna get one with this lot.

Bet At least I can do 'em. I'm not like you. At least I know the bloody answers. You'd be no good, you don't know anything.

Al That's true that is, you're right there.

Bet You don't know anything.

Al I don't know why I married you.

Bet You think you're so funny, don't you?

Al You make the answers up half the time.

Bet I don't.

Al How much do you spend on them bloody magazines?

Bet That's got nowt to do with you, that, that's my pocket money, I do what I want with it.

Al Oh shuddup.

Bet You shuddup.

Black-out

The Lights come up. Days later. Bet and Al change positions

Al Do you want a coffee?
Bet No.
Al I'll make one ...
Bet I don't want one.
Al Oh, right.
Bet Thanks.
Al I'll not have one then.
Bet You can have one for me ...
Al It's not worth putting the kettle on for, is it?
Bet You have one, I don't want one.
Al Why don't you want one?
Bet Why do you want one?
Al Sommat to do.
Bet I don't fancy a coffee, you have one. I'm not stopping you from having
　　one.
Al No point me having one, is there?

Pause

Bet There's nowt good ont telly tonight.
Al We could watch the test card for a bit.
Bet I've seen it.

Al begins to prowl the white box

Al This bloody house, I wish it'd blow up.
Bet You don't.
Al I wish the whole lot would blow up.
Bet I wish you'd blow up. Pheeew bang, all over. Head all across the
　　ceiling, bits of chest on the telly, stomach on the wall, limbs out of the
　　window, floating about somewhere. I wish you'd blow up.
Al I might go to bed.
Bet Go then.
Al I think I'll have a bath ...
Bet There's no water.
Al What?

Bet There's no hot water.

Al Why?

Bet I've had a bath.

Al When?

Bet When I came in from work. I had a soak because my feet were killing
me so I had a soak.

Al Oh right.

Bet I had the water right up to the top and all. I had a right good soak.

Al No bloody hot water now.

Bet Right up to the rim I had it.

Al It should've drowned you.

Bet It was nearly coming over, you should've seen me. And bubble bath,
I had some of that green bubble bath, there was just a bit left so I had all
suds. Ooh I looked like a bloody film star just laid there, soaking.

Al Who do you think you are?

Bet I love to soak.

Al It ruins that bath.

Bet It doesn't.

Al It leaves a mark on the bath.

Bet It doesn't.

Al It does.

Bet You're the one who leaves a mark around the bath.

Al I do not.

Bet You do, I don't tell you, but I clean up after you. Every time you get
a bath there's a line of scum left around the bath. It's like your skin's
peeling off. I have to get a cloth and scrape it off. I've done that and not
told you for ten years.

Al I'll start using bubble bath.

Bet And you never stand on the bath mat. You leave these two great big
sodden footprints on the carpet. You never do anything you're supposed
to.

Al I think I'll make myself a sandwich.

Bet Another? You've had a dozen today.

Al I've got to eat sommat, at least I'm not lounging about all day in the
bloody bath.

Bet You're only one grunt short of being a pig.

Al Well, if I'm a pig what are you?

Bet At least I like a laugh. You never want to do anything.

Al I do.

Bet I look at you sometimes and I wonder. We're only here once and look
    what I've ended up with.

Al Why don't you leave then?

Bet I might do.

Al I've heard that before.

Bet I did all sorts before I met you. I had a good life before I met you.

Al Leave then. Go back to your dad, see if he wants you.

Bet You're useless around the house. You can't cook. I have to do
    everything.

Al Why do you stay then?

Bet I don't know. Ten years.

Al Nine.

Bet Ten years in September. I wish I'd never said "I do" sometimes.

Al You silly woman.

Bet Ten years and nothing to show for it except you.

Black-out

*The Lights come up. Months later. Both are as they were earlier, but
Bet is elated and jumping about*

Bet Ha ha, you're wrong aren't you, admit it, admit it, for once in your
    life, admit it.

Al What are you on about?

Bet Admit that you're wrong, then I'll tell you.

Al All right I'm wrong, what is it?

Bet Read that ... no, second thoughts, I'll read it.

Al What is it?

Bet Ha ha, listen to this.

Al Read it then.

Bet (*reading from a letter*) "Dear Guest." That's me.

Al Get on with it.

Bet (*reading*) "Dear Guest, We are delighted to announce that you are a
    lucky winner of our Romantic Break Competition. Take you and your
    loved one", I suppose that's you,"for a night to Romantic Paris."

Al Bloody hell.

Bet (*reading*) "Travel overnight in luxury on North Sea Ferries, all
    expenses paid, and stay at the delightful Saint Germain Hotel. Return
    journey on North Sea Ferries rounds off your unforgettable Romantic
    Break."

Al Bloody hell.

Bet What do you think?

Al Bloody hell.

Bet All we have to do is find our spending money.

Al I knew there'd be a catch.

Bet Admit that you're wrong about these competitions. 'S not a fix is it?

Al You won't be able to have time off work, will you?

Bet Course I will.

Al Might not have a job when you come back.

Bet Oh God, give me strength. Don't you think it's great? I've always wanted to go to Paris, haven't you? Don't you think it's great? Are you pleased?

Al Who are you going to go with?

Bet You.

Al I can't go.

Bet Why?

Al Well I can't.

Bet I don't believe you.

Al I don't want to be trailing around France, do I. Why don't you take Rita?

Bet All right then, I'll take Rita.

Al And I hate boats.

Bet You've never been on one.

Al There's no way I'd sleep on a boat. I mean what if it's rough? It'd probably sink with my luck. You and Rita go. I'm serious, you and Rita go and have a good time. I'll only ruin it, you know that ... Besides, I haven't got a passport.

Bet I haven't.

Al I've got nothing to wear.

Bet Well, that's never been a problem before, has it? We'll need to buy a new case, we can't take that one we've got, it looks a mess. I think I'll need a new suit.

Al We're only going for one day.

Bet I thought you weren't coming?

Al I'll go for you.

Bet No, it's OK, I'll go with Rita. I know you don't like boats. You stay here in your shed, you'll only spoil it. I'll go with Rita, she'll be gob-smacked when I tell her that you want her to go instead of you. Me and Rita in Paris, oooh là là ... We'll have a dirty weekend, I might come back with a sexy French bloke. I'll nip around and tell her.

Al Bugger Rita.

Bet No, it's OK, I understand. You've never been away and you don't want to go. That's OK. Anyway, I don't want to be seen going around Paris with you.

Al Once you start gallivanting off ...

Bet I wonder if Rita's got a passport.

Al Once you get there you might not want to come back.

Bet I won't want to come back to you.

Al You can't speak a work of French.

Bet I can buy a book.

Al Probably get mugged.

Bet I can't wait.

Al I think you should think about it.

Bet I have thought about it.

Al I'm not going.

Bet Yeah, I know, great. I'm going and you're not, and that's that. I'll go with Rita.

Black-out

> *During the black-out Bet exits. Al moves the chairs to the back wall and exits*

The doorway of the white box becomes a doorway on a ship. The door is hinged and closed, with a porthole

Music plays: Jacques Brel's "Vesoul". The Lights come up

> *Al dances on with a large lifebuoy, hangs it from the back wall, and exits*

> *Bet dances on carrying a suitcase. We see her look at the size of the ship in front of her. A light picks her out*

Bet Wooow ... I can't believe it ... I can't believe I'm doing it ... I feel like I'm going to burst open with excitement. And the ferry, you should see the size of the ferry! It's massive. I've never seen anything as big in my life. And I can't move for people, people everywhere. A sea of faces and suitcases, cars, buses from all over the place. School parties, tall Dutch kids, a party of pensioners from Newcastle, French students. Everyone is excited to be going back home or abroad like me. I feel free, for the first time in years I feel like I'm game for a laugh, I feel like I can fly. I don't know where *he* is, and I'm not bothered. I've packed everything, passport, travellers' cheques, phrase book, I've packed myself a suit in case I go anywhere. Nice. (She *picks up her case and walks around the stage*)

The spot goes off

Al enters with a suitcase

Al Look out, women and children first.
Bet Oh you're here, are you?
Al I've been talking to one of the crew. I went to school with him.
Bet It's jam-packed full this ferry.
Al I hope it's not too heavy. It might sink.
Bet Well you'd better get off, then.
Al Is this the right boat?
Bet You should be on that one. Rotterdam.
Al There's a disco.
Bet I know.
Al Two bars.
Bet Don't go mad, you.
Al Great int it?
Bet Giz a cuddle then.
Al Why, are you cold?
Bet Yeah.
Al Put a cardigan on.
Bet I don't like the look of them lifeboats.
Al They're all right.
Bet What number are we?
Al Five-one sommat ...
Bet Right.
Al I hope I can sleep.
Bet I don't want the top bunk.
Al Have you brought the Sealegs?
Bet You can have the top bunk.
Al What if I fall off, I'll kill you.
Bet I've got about ten Sealegs.

Al Is that enough?

Bet How many do you want?

Al It's going to be windy, I think.

Bet It'll be all right.

Al Will it?

Bet These boats sail every night.

Al Not with us on it.

Bet It'll be all right. I checked on the telly, it said it was going to be a calm crossing.

Al I looked and it said moderate.

Bet Calm it said.

Al I'm not arguing ...

Bet It said calm.

Al It said moderate.

Bet Yeah, well, that's what it'll be.

Al Ar, but what do you call moderate?

Bet Moderate.

Al Ar, what's moderate?

Bet Moderate's like calm, isn't it?

Al Is it?

Bet Course it is.

Al I don't know if I should take any notice of you. You don't know owt.

Bet Look, try and find the cabin. (*She indicates the suitcase*) Take this. I'll meet you down on D Deck.

Al D Deck, where's that?

Bet Find it.

Al Ay ay, Captain.

He exits, taking the cases with him

We hear a voice-over

Voice Attention, Austroblitz, dinner is now being served in the restaurant on C Deck. Families and coach parties may now dine.

Al enters

Al and Bet sit together on chairs UR

Bet Massive restaurant, int it?

Al Not much ... it's like a bloody hotel.

Bet That's what it is, a floating hotel.

Al I don't like sitting with other people.

Bet Well, what do you want us to do — have dinner in the cabin?

Al I mean here like this, with these others. We're too close.

Bet They're a nice couple. They work in Hull at the University.

Al Where are they going?

Bet France.

Al Oh. Like us.

Bet Yeah.

Al Have they won it?

Bet No.

Al Look at all these people.

Bet They're going to a little village. Bolougne sommat. They're taking their car to a gîte ...

Al Why, what's wrong with it?

Bet Oh, don't start with your jokes.

Al We should've kept the car.

Bet We'll get another one day.

Al We should've gone away for a few days in England.

Bet Yeah.

Al Yeah.

Bet Where?

Al Well, we could have had a couple of days at loggerheads.

Bet You.

Al What ...

Bet You think you're funny.

Al And I'll tell you sommat you didn't know.

Bet What?

Al There's a nudist beach at Filey.

Bet There isn't?

Al There is.

Bet Look shurrup, people can hear you ...

Al There is.

Bet What do you want when they come — soup or fruit juice?

Al There is.

Bet People can hear you.

Al There's a nudist beach at Filey, but you can't see a lot according to form, because they all lay on their fronts. But there's plenty of room to park a bike, apparently.

Bet I bet they're French.

Al Where?

Bet Over there ...

Al They're not French are they?

Bet Well, they're having wine.

Al Look at that lot there. They're having curry but they're not from India, are they? You do talk some rubbish at times.

Bet What are you having?

Al What is there?

Bet Salad bar.

Al Oh, I'll have a salad then.

Bet Or there's curry ...

Al I right fancy curry, it looks nice.

Bet And I think there's chicken pie and chips.

Al Chicken pie, has it got mushrooms in it?

Bet How do I know?

Al I don't know what to have ... Can you have as much as you want?

Bet I think so.

Al Right then. (*He freezes*)

Bet I want to die when he goes to the chef three times. Curry, pie and salad and each portion heaped up on his plate, and him smiling like a buffoon. Showing the rest of the ship what he was going to eat.

Al Bloody lovely that. I'll tell you sommat, there's some silly sods on here only having one meal. I mean we've paid for it, ant we?

Bet No.

Al Well, it's there, isn't it? They'll only chuck it to the seagulls if nobody eats it.

Bet I didn't know where to look.

Al What's up now, we're supposed to be on holiday, aren't we? I've got some cheese for later, in case we get a bit peckish during the night.

Bet He had helped himself to half a pound of Edam which he'd wrapped up in a serviette and stuffed in his pocket.

Al I could get some more if you want it?

Bet We walk along the plush corridors of the boat, and I detect in the air a faint smell of sick which is a reminder that we are at sea.

Al It's not bad is it?

Bet You should've brought a sketch pad, you could have drawn some of this.

Al Why? You've got a camera, haven't you?

Bet Do you want to see a film?

Al No, I had a look earlier. You have to travel backwards. I don't like that.

Bet Have you never been on a train?

Al Let's get a drink in ... (*He turns and freezes*)

Bet On D Deck the lounge looks like something from a feature film. I could just imagine voyages in the past. Ships full of barons and countesses all making their way around the world to seek fame and fortune. Everyone dressed for dinner in tuxedo and tie, instead of trainers and T-shirts.

Al I'm having a pint. What do you want?

Al brings down the chairs and they sit

Bet We sit in a secluded corner just behind the bar.

Al Smooth ride, int it. Brilliant. I could get used to this. Hope it stays like this all night. It's as smooth as a baby's arse.

Bet Don't be sick, will you.

Al I've had a Sealeg.

Bet Just take it steady.

Al I'm only having a pint.

Bet Right.

Al What do you want?

Bet Can I have a white wine?

Al A bit French, int it?

Bet Well, what did you expect, we're on holiday, aren't we?

Al I might have a pint and a chaser, is it all free?

Bet No.

Al I'll just have a pint then. (*He moves* R *and freezes*)

We hear soft piano music: "Love Story" and "Moon River"

Bet Over by the window the pianist tickles her way through "Precious Moments" ... and she chatters and plays requests but no-one really listens except me, and I applaud, and I feel really good. Like I was born for this sort of life instead of selling training shoes.

Al She's killing them songs.

Bet She's good.

Al Shall I ask her to play Phil Collins?

Bet No, leave it. Let's work out what we're going to see, shall we?

Al Right then. Let's have a plan.

Bet Let's not have a plan. Let's just see what there is and if we don't see it all we can go back again.

Al When?

Bet Another time.

Al Well, we've got to see the Eiffel Tower, ant we?

Bet See it, we've got to go up it. We've got tickets.

Al We haven't got to go up it, have we?

Bet I thought we'd do all the sights on the first day and then we could just relax on the coming back.

Al If we do all the sights on the first day we'll need to. How will we go on with eating?

Bet What do you mean?

Al I mean, what if there's nowt we like?

Bet You like bread, don't you?

Al Yeah. (*He has a small tourist guide to Paris and looks through it*)

Bet Well, there's always bread. They make really nice bread.

Al Arch de Triomphe — we'll want to see that. And the Gare du Nord.

Bet That's a station.

Al How do you know?

Bet Because I've been looking at it every night for the last month.

Al All right, Marco Polo, keep your shirt on.

Bet We'll have to bring mi mam sommat back. And I said I'd bring Rita sommat.

Al We want some duty free and all.

Bet We'll get some. And we'll have a saunter down the Champs-Elysées.

Al What is there?

Bet Shops.

Al Great.

Bet Why, what do you want to see?

Al Well, I wouldn't mind looking at that Pigalle.

Bet What for?

Al See what it's like. I heard some bus drivers talking about it down in that shop. They said it was an interesting place to go.

Bet Oh yeah. I know you.

Al They said they always take bus trips there. (*Pause*) Must be interesting, if they always go.

Bet Well, there's nowt there.

Al How do you know?

Bet Well, it's all sex shops and all that, int it?

Al Is it?

Bet You know it is.

Al No, I didn't. I didn't know what it was.

Bet I mean we don't want to be going all the way to Paris to look at sex shops, do we?

Al No, suppose not.

Bet I mean there's lots more to see. Opéra. Louvre.

Al Oh yeah, opera, great.

Bet Napoleon's Tomb. Notre Dame.

Al We can see if that hunchback's in.

Bet Pompidou Centre, there's loads. We don't want to be spending our time looking at sex shops.

Al They're sex-mad over there, you know. I should watch 'em. One of the lads had been, at work. He said you couldn't move up there for prostitutes and them transvestites.

Bet Well, if you want to go, you go, but I'm not.

Al No, I don't want to go, I was only saying.

Bet Look, this looks good, Montmartre, Artists' Quarter ... You'd like that. You might be able to teach 'em a thing or two.

Al Ha ha ...

Bet Oh and by the way, it says everybody tips the waiters and all ...

Al I tip.

Bet Oh yeah.

Al I do.

Bet When ever have you tipped anybody?

Al I can't remember, when I last went out.

Bet Well, shut up then.

Al How long is it on the bus when we get there?

Bet Three hours.

Al Three hours?

Bet What's wrong with that?

Al Nowt.

Pause

Bet Typical of you, that, int it?

Al What?

Bet Wanting to look at sex shops.

Al It doesn't bother me.

Bet Three hours and then we're there. You'll be all right on the bus, it'll
suit you.

Al Why?

Bet There's a toilet and a video. It's all you need, int it?

Al Where's the hotel?

Bet How do I know, I haven't been there before, have I?

Al I thought you said you'd been studying the map?

Bet Bloody sex shops? You ought to go learn sommat. They reckon that
Frenchmen are the best lovers in Europe.

Al There's a toilet on the coach is there? That's handy.

Pause

Bet She's good on that piano, int she?

Al She's going through me.

Bet Oh, you've had a drink, have you?

Al Yeah, I have, and I'm having another. Do you want one?

Bet No, I'm all right with one glass of wine.

Al You're not going to make that last all night, are you?

Bet Why?

Al Well, it's embarrassing, int it? Have another.

Bet It's not. It's what normal people do.

Al I'm normal.

Bet Are you?

Al Don't start it.

Bet I'm not, I'm just being reasonable.

Al So can I have another pint or what?

Bet You don't have to ask me.

Al I do.

Bet You don't.

Al Right. I'm having another pint then.

Bet Have one then.

Al I'll be all right, I mean, I'm not going to get legless, am I?

Bet Aren't you? That'd make a change then.

Al I'll not have one, then!

Bet A smooth ride, int it?

Al No wonder, is there.

Bet Why?

Al We're still in Hull. The barman told us. We're waiting for some cargo to arrive from Goole.

Bet Oh, it must be delayed because of the fog.

Al Fog, what fog?

Bet Fog on the M62.

Al Well, I hope it's not going to follow us. That's all we want, to be lost at sea.

Bet I hope he shuts them doors properly. I was sat here thinking we were nearly in France.

Al Well we're not, we're in Hull.

Bet You don't think it'll be foggy out at sea, do you?

Al How do I know?

Bet How can they see in the fog?

Al The captain's a rabbit.

Bet You're not funny.

Al You'll be all right, get some wine down you.

Bet I don't want a lot. I tell you what, I'll go and play on the fruit machines and then I'll go to the disco, I right fancy a dance.

Al Well, I'm not dancing with you.

Bet So what's new?

Al I'm having another pint.

Bet That's it, go and get legless, you'll be sick.

Al Shut up and go and have a dance will you?

A sudden burst of music. Disco Lights come up DL. *Al stands upstage. A spotlight picks him out as Bet dances to the music*

Down in the disco, I stand like an island watching her parade about. She's enjoying herself, she's having a good time, I'm glad about that. I wish I could join in, I do, I wish I could get up there with her but sommat stops me, I just stand watching 'em all dance, and I'm rooted to the spot, my feet are in concrete, and I'm jealous to death. She's not bothered, she's the oldest one dancin' but she's not bothered, now she's dancin' with some French students, and now she's with a tall Dutch kid — he's only about fifteen, look at her, she's loving it. Look at me, I'm pathetic. I look at a young lass from Antwerp, and I get stupid ideas, I'm thirty-eight, let's be honest, so I tap my foot so as not to look too sad. (*To Bet*) Enjoying it?

Bet Brilliant.
Al I'm going to have another, do you want one?
Bet No, I'm all right, I'm dancing.
Al Bloody hell.
Bet Int it brilliant?
Al An hour later she's still dancin' and the boat rocks, and dips and we
   are out there, out into the North Sea, out into all that blackness.
Bet I feel a bit queasy.
Al What?
Bet I feel a bit queasy.
Al There's no wonder, is there? I thought you were having a stroke.
Bet What?
Al It was a joke, the way you were dancing.
Bet I fancy a bit of fresh air.
Al Have you seen the time?
Bet Come on, let's go on deck.
Al It's windy out there.
Bet Oh come on, you fart, let's live a bit.
Al I thought you felt queasy.
Bet Let's get some fresh air, I'm boiling.

*The Lights change. The disco music fades. Wind is heard as the Lights
go to blue out on deck. A cloud effect gives a sense of movement*

   Bet exits and immediately returns with two windjammers

Al brings the chairs c. *Both Al and Bet reach for the windjammers
which they try and put on against the wind. Al reaches up and sets the
hanging light swinging to give the impression of the boat's movement.
The wind fades*

   Put your coat on ...
Al It's only plastic.
Bet Windy.
Al Windy ... is that an understatement?
Bet This'll blow the cobwebs off us.
Al It'll blow us off if we don't watch it.
Bet It's a bit scary, int it?
Al Do you feel any better?

Bet A bit ... it was too stuffy. I haven't danced like that in years.

Al Nobody has.

Bet I want fresh air.

Al Well, it doesn't come any fresher than this.

Bet It's great ...

Al Look at the waves.

Bet This doesn't look calm to me ...

Al No , it dunt look calm to me either. In fact I'd say it looks bloody rough ... look out for the icebergs.

Bet Moderate to rough?

Al I suppose so.

Bet Bloody hell. I hope it doesn't get much rougher.

Al Well, I think it will.

Bet How do you know?

Al There's a forecast on the wall near that Information Desk. A weather chart thing.

Bet Oh yeah ...

Al It said that erratic winds were expected to come down from Poland, and cause havoc in the North Sea. That's why I've had all that to drink — if it gets bad I'm gonna sleep through it.

Bet Why didn't you tell me?

Al Why, you don't feel sick do you?

Bet Shall we go back?

Al What for? We're all right just yet. Just take deep breaths if you feel bad.

Bet Let's go back.

Al You're all right. Nothing to be frightened of. Whooo, I'll tell you what, all this fresh air's making me a bit woozy. Whooo, brilliant. God, look at the clouds.

Bet Where?

Al Where? There in the bloody sky. Look at the clouds. Frightening.

Bet It's going to be stormy.

Pause

Al Look at the clouds.

Pause

Bet Don't go too near the edge, will you? Be dead easy for somebody to fall off, wouldn't it?

Al Yeah.

Bet Just don't go near the edge.

Al How do you feel?

Bet Sick.

Al Take deep breaths from your mouth.

Bet Thanks. (*She breathes deeply*)

Al Better?

Bet No.

Al Just keep breathing.

Bet Yeah.

Al Do you want me to hold you?

Bet No, I want you to leave me alone. Oh dear ... have I gone pale?

Al Pale green, yeah.

Bet Oh dear ....

Al Just keep breathing.

Bet Don't you feel bad?

Al I do a bit.

Bet You shouldn't've had all that food. I knew you'd be sick.

Al Give it a rest for a minute, will you?

Bet You were like a bloody animal, I didn't know where to look.

Al Ohhh, I feel bad.

Bet I've got no sympathy.

Al I need a pee.

Bet Let's go back then.

Al No ... I'll have to have one out.

Bet Don't be pathetic ...

Al Nobody'll know.

Bet I will.

Al I'll have one over the side.

Bet You won't.

Al It must be all the water.

Bet Oh yeah, it'll not be the beer, will it? You always have to overdo it.

Al Now we know what moderate is.

Bet I feel a bit bad again.

Al Did you have a Sealeg?

Bet There was one left.

Al You should've had a brandy. That's supposed to calm your stomach.

Bet Oh ...

Al Are you all right?

Bet No, I feel awful.
Al Do you feel sick?
Bet Yeah.
Al I feel all right now.
Bet I'm going to be sick.
Al Keep swallowing.
Bet I am.
Al What do you want me to do?
Bet Oh hell ... I think I'm gonna ...
Al Are you all right?

Bet makes her way to the side of the boat upstage and heaves off stage

Bet Uuurrrrrghgh ...
Al Are you all right?
Bet Uuurghhhhhh ...
Al Oh dear.
Bet Urghhhhhhhh ...
Al Speak up when you're through.
Bet Uuuurghhhhh ...
Al Get it up, it'll be better once it's up.
Bet Oh, I hate being sick.
Al I do.
Bet Urgghghghhhh ...
Al You're making me feel bad.
Bet Don't help me, will you?
Al What do you want me to do?
Bet (*recovering from sea sickness*) Oh ...
Al All right.
Bet I felt fine then it just came.
Al I don't know, I can't take you anywhere, can I?
Bet Oh ... typical.
Al What?
Bet Nothing ever happens to you, does it?
Al You're joking, aren't you?
Bet Oh, I feel better.
Al What have you been eating?
Bet It must be them chocolates. I tret myself to some chocolates before
we got on. For a little treat.

Al You and them treats. You didn't offer me one.

Bet It was my treat.

Al Serves you right then.

Bet God's judgement on me.

Al You feel OK, can I get you owt?

Bet No.

Al Better?

Bet (*recovering*) That's a lot better.

Al It sounded like it ...

Bet One good thing, I've still got my own teeth ...

Al It's a good job, int it, otherwise they'd be in Holland by now.

Bet Is it calming down?

Al Feel better?

Bet Yeah. This is with you.

Al What?

Bet Wanting to come out here in this weather ...

Al You wanted some fresh air, I was happy enough watching the disco.

Bet Let's go back. I want to read for a bit. (*She moans*)

Al Oh ... go then ... I'm going to stay out here.

Bet I can't leave you out here, can I?

Al Why, what am I gonna do, jump off?

Bet Oh, don't start ...

Al I know you'll never understand, but I feel ashamed.

Bet Ashamed? What, of behaving like a pig? You do it all the time.

Al Of this holiday. Everybody on here's paid and we're here for free.

Bet So what?

Al I haven't taken you on holiday for two years and the only holiday we have is one that we've won.

Bet It doesn't matter.

Al Course it matters.

Bet There's nothing wrong with winning.

Al I've always wanted to take you somewhere nice, and we go and win a bloody holiday. I mean, where have we been before? Grange-over-Sands in a holiday flat and you hated it.

Bet It doesn't matter.

Al What's going to happen next year?

Bet Next year'll be different.

Al Will it? What are you gonna win next year?

Bet What's wrong with you? Just enjoy it.

Al Or the year after that ... because you know we can't afford to go away.
   And that's why you do them competitions — to get back at me.
Bet I don't.
Al You do.
Bet Let's take a day at a time.
Al I've got nowt to look forward to, have I?
Bet Give it a miss, will you?
Al Bloody nowt.
Bet Stop feeling sorry for yourself and grow up.
Al Do you want to know sommat?
Bet Go on ...
Al I'm fed up ...
Bet Well, throw yourself overboard then, and end it all.
Al Do you think I haven't thought about it?
Bet Do it then. You're too scared to do it.
Al I will do it and then you'd be in a mess.
Bet Would I?
Al You would.
Bet I wouldn't.
Al What a bloody country we live in. We've had a win a bloody holiday.
Bet So do thousands of others. It's not just me and you. Can we forget this
   and go inside? I'm frozen.
Al You go, I'm stopping here. (*Pause*) Go then, go and read a book.
   (*Pause; shouting*) It's my holiday — I want to do what I want.
Bet Oh, I could just push you off this boat and think I'd done nowt ... Push
   you off and start my life again. You'd be down there floating about with
   a belly full of beer.
Al (*seeing a light at sea*) England.
Bet What?
Al England there, look at it. Just an island int it? I don't think it'll ever get
   sorted out now.
Bet It's not our worry, is it?
Al No ... Have you looked at the people lately? Have you looked at the
   people in the streets? Don't you think they look sad?
Bet Not as sad as you.
Al I think they look sad.
Bet I wish you'd never come.
Al I know.
Bet I wish I'd come with Rita.

Al I told you to. But you never listen to me.
Bet You spoil everything.
Al I've never done anything right for you, have I? Not in ten years.
Bet Let's go back inside, we can't talk about this here.

Pause

Al Come here ...
Bet No ...
Al Come here, you ...
Bet No ...
Al Come here, it's a holiday.

Bet goes to Al and they hug. He looks at her

Al Sorry.
Bet What for?

Pause. In the silence they place the chairs back to back c and sit sideways on them so that they are facing the audience

Al For going on ...
Bet It's OK.
Al Do you want to know sommat?
Bet What?
Al Your breath stinks of sick ...

A beat

Bet Thanks.

Pause. Al attempts to put his arm around Bet. Finally she succumbs

Al (*excited*) Paris ... bloody hell.

French music plays: "Les Bourgeois" by Jacques Brel and Jean Corti. As the music plays the Lights fade, and just before the Lights reach black-out Al waves goodbye to England

Black-out

ACT II

A large Renoir painting fills the entire stage. Two Parisian chairs are placed UR. They are the only props used in Paris, and can fold away. The hanging light is no longer visible

Can-can music plays as Bet and Al enter and sit on the chairs. They are tired from looking around. They do not take in the audience yet. The music stops

Al I'm tired out. I mean, we've walked all over.

Bet Well, I told you we should have got the Métro.

Al I'm not getting no Métro.

Bet Why?

Al People get mugged on the Métro.

Bet They don't.

Al People get mugged.

Bet They don't.

Al They do.

Bet Millions of people use it every day ...

Al Ar, and some of 'em get mugged.

Bet Bloody hell, you ...

Al It's bigger than I thought it would be ...

Bet Ar, it's bigger than your shed, int it?

Al Just about ...

Bet What do you think to the hotel?

Al Not bad, and two toilets, that's handy ...

Bet It's a bidet ...

Al I know ...

Bet And that champagne in our room was great, wasn't it? I'll take that home. (*She takes in the audience*) We're up by the Trocadéro, from here you can see the Eiffel Tower.

Al You can see the Eiffel Tower from anywhere.

Bet And the Seine.

Al Can't move for kids. Are we going to have a bite? (*He brings the chairs* DR)

Bet He doesn't want to sit outside the café, so despite the soaring heat we go and sit inside the Café Trocadéro ... We gaze up at the large menu on the wall ...

Al And we settle near a posh French bloke who's eating an omelette.

Bet Do you want an omelette?

They sit on two chairs, giving the impression that the restaurant is full. They are pleased at being in the restaurant

Al The menu is all in French.

Bet What did you expect?

Al Well, I thought ...

Bet Nice, int it?

Al It's all rate, yeah.

Bet Ohhh, my feet. I'm ready for this. Ohhh.

Al You choose sommat for me, I can't follow it.

Bet Let's have sommat daring, shall we? Can you see what there is?

Al I can hardly see the wall.

Bet You need some new glasses, I've told you.

Al If you can't tell what it says we can have a Big Mac.

Bet I read the menu and make out something about fish and steak. I think. It'll be a laugh, we'll have steak and fish. Int it nice?

Al What about an omelette?

Bet It doesn't say omelette.

Al He's got an omelette.

Bet Take your pick, fish or steak.

Al Is that all there is?

Bet You can have soup.

Al I'll have steak. Well done, you never know what you're eating. Where's the loo?

Bet How do I know?

Al (*whispering*) I'll try and find the loo. Hey, look at that — they've got a different menu to us. They've got a different menu to us! Crafty sods, I bet you can have omelette on that menu.

Bet Have steak now.

Al Crafty sods, one menu for them and one for the tourists. That'd never happen in England.

Bet Go to the toilet.

Al I right fancy an omelette. Shall I say sommat?

Bet You're having steak. Make do with that.
Al Crafty sods. (*To the waiter*) Hey, I say, mate ... (*He whistles*)
Bet Go to the toilet and leave it.
Al Crafty sods.
Bet I thought you were going to try and be romantic?
Al I am trying.

Al walks upstage looking for the toilet, which he finds is simply a hole in the ground. During the following, Bet and Al address the audience separately

Bet So he's in the loo, and I try through smiles and points to order. (*To an imaginary waiter*) Bonjour. Une Steak Tartare. Une poisson and sauce. With two cups of tea. Tea ... please tea ... merci. And all the while I'm struggling with my little book and bad grammar, I know and he knows that the waiter speaks better English than uz. "Merci," he snaps, a bit over-friendly like, and floats away to a table where he is relieved to serve someone French. And I hope I've ordered the right thing, and I sit and watch and dread his return from la toilette.

Al In le toilet I'm confused. I've wandered down two flights of stairs to get here and when I've arrived all I see is a hole in the ground, and two foot pads.

Bet Around the café I catch polite glances and smiles and whispers which I translate into "she's English", followed by a little laugh. And every Chanel suit and elegant two piece is looking at me.

Al And I still stand, looking, looking at this hole in the earth.

Bet The men draw on their Gauloises, and the women sip their muscadet and chat and laugh and smoke, and I can't believe that I'm in Paris, this is the colour and excitement of a wonderful city. And I dread his return. More women enter the café, slim, elegant women, expensive women and the intoxication draws me into an insecurity. They look at me and know something is wrong. They seem to know I don't belong, and I think I hear them say that my suit is from British Home Stores.

Al I stand still, silent, thinking, pondering. I wait for a while, I go through the motions in my head. I make it appear as if I've been, I time myself in my head. But there is no way. The hole in the ground still beckons, but I can't oblige.

Bet And suddenly I'm desperate for him to return, he's been there too long, he always takes too long. Too many eyes now, too many slanting

smiles, lip corners twist, and necks crane to look at me, and why doesn't
he come back? What can he be doing in there? And then the meal arrives.
Mine a beautiful piece of fish cooked in white wine with a sauce to
match, too nice to eat really, his a plate of raw mince meat with a raw
egg in the middle.

Al I make my way back up the spiral staircase, stunned and slightly
worried.

Al returns to the table

Bet Where've you been?
Al Wait till you have to go. (*He looks at the steak*) I look at the plate of
raw meat.
Bet Get it.
Al What is it?
Bet Just don't make a fuss, I didn't know, just eat it, everybody's looking.
Al There's no wonder, is there? I've got some horse's giblets on my plate.
Bet Just get it.
Al I can't eat this, I wouldn't give it to a pig.
Bet I thought you were hungry.
Al What are you trying to do, kill me?
Bet Just eat it. I'm sorry, all right I didn't know what it was.
Al I don't know what it is.
Bet For goodness sake, eat it, we can't send it back, can we?
Al And so I eat it. Cold raw mince meat. I eat it. I mix the egg into the mince
and eat it. Slowly I can feel the meat fighting its way to my stomach. The
egg eases its way down, a little hiccup (*He hiccups*), a moment of panic,
a worry, a serviette wipes a bubble from my lips. But all is secure. A sip
of tea and it's all gone. I eat it all. I'm so hungry I could eat it again. And
the man with the omelette looks enviously at my empty plate. I wipe my
mouth and sip my English tea. (*He belches loudly*) Ah ... nice ...
Bet Don't.
Al That's what they do over here.
Bet (*standing up to leave*) With some relief we depart.
Al Bon voyage. (*He takes the chairs* UR)
Bet And after l'addition, he leaves a tip.
Al Hey, keep away from mucky women.
Bet And out on to the streets. The noisy, busy streets.
Al We stand on the Place de Trocadéro and take in the sights.

Bet We've nearly done 'em all ...

Al Great.

Bet In just under six hours.

Al It must be a record. (*A pause while he looks out at the sights*) Place de la Concorde over there, Invalides, been there. Up there, Arc de Triomphe.

Bet Do you like it?

Al Well, it's different, int it?

Bet But do you like it?

Al Yeah, course I do.

Bet Let's go up the Eiffel Tower.

Al What for?

Bet Soo Paris.

Al We can see it from here.

Bet Oh come on, come on, please ... We've got tickets.

Al Do you want to?

Bet Yeah, come on. Everybody goes up the Tower.

Al So we queue for thirty minutes in front of a school party from Plymouth who talk non-stop about some French girls they have met, and Madonna, and I pretend to be foreign, and these kids giggle and push, and the only thing I hope is that they are not in our lift because if they are I'll swing for 'em. There's only one thing I hate more than kids ... and it's heights.

Bet We agree, as is the compromise of my life, that we won't go right to the top. And on the first station I buy my mother a flag with the Tower on.

Al Where's she gunna put that?

Bet He buys a model of the Tower in a snow storm.

Al It's cheap but I like it.

Bet And there we are, over-looking a jigsaw of beauty.

They stand c. Bet looks out towards the audience

Bet What a view — hey, get that painted.

Al Look at that ... All the streets are in straight lines.

Bet That's to stop another revolution, int it? You could get a tank down them streets.

Al Bloody hell.

Bet I'm not thick.

Al I know that. (*He moves away*)

Bet Great tower, int it?

Al (*looking elsewhere*) Three hundred metres high.

Bet Really?

Al It was built as part of the World's Fair. To celebrate the centenary of the Revolution.

Bet Hey ...

Al What?

Bet Look at us in Paris.

Al They were going to demolish it in nineteen-o-nine.

Bet That's not true, is it?

Al Course it is.

Bet How come you know all this?

Al It says so here on this plaque. (*Reading*) "It is a unique masterpiece of equilibrium and lightness despite weighing seven thousand tons."

Bet Look at you.

Al What?

Bet You're enjoying it, aren't you?

Al Why do you put up with me?

Bet Answer me. Are you enjoying it?

Al Yeah.

Bet Well, why don't you tell me?

Al I do.

Bet You don't, you think you do, you think you talk to me and tell me things but you don't. You keep it inside.

Al Where shall we go next?

Bet I thought you'd seen enough.

Al Come on, tourist guide, take us somewhere.

Bet Give us a kiss then, in Paris.

Al What for?

Bet Because the tourist guide needs one.

Al No.

Bet I'll throw you off the Tower if you don't.

Al politely pecks her on the cheek

   Well, thanks a lot.

Al You're welcome.

Bet Your breath smells awful.

Al I'm not surprised, it's them horse giblets.

Bet I don't know how women can resist you.

The Lights change to indicate the Louvre. The Mona Lisa is simply a power white light pointing downward

Al After the Tower we nip across to the Louvre. (*He sees something*) Woow, look at that ...

Bet What?

Al Woow ...

Bet Calm down ... everybody's looking ...

Al Bloody hell.

Bet Haven't you seen it before?

Al Not in real life ... (*To the audience*) Mona Lisa.

Bet Small, int it?

Al Look at it.

Bet I thought it would be bigger.

Al (*breathlessly*) It's fantastic.

Bet Small, int it?

Al Ohhh God, it's brilliant.

Bet I didn't think you'd like it, I thought you'd say it was rubbish.

Al But just look at it, look at the colour. I've never seen owt like it.

Bet It's no better than the others to me.

Al Oh, you're joking. It's a masterpiece.

Bet What makes it better then?

Al Look at the colours. See them others, same period. But they're very crude compared to this. You see that smile, wherever you stand it looks like she's smiling at you.

Bet She is smiling at me ...

Al She was a whore, wan't she?

Bet Was she?

Al At first they thought she was an official's wife.

Bet You're good, aren't you?

Al But they reckon she was a bit of a goer.

Bet That's why she's smiling?

Al He's tried to blend all the colours, you see, like smoke. Bloody hell, it's brilliant.

Bet You couldn't do that, then?

Al Not in a million years.

Bet Keep trying.

Al I will do.

Bet (*turning, pointing to another painting*) I like that one, and that one. Oh, and I like that one.

They look at the art

Al Renoir, and Manet.

Bet And that one, and that one.

Al Cézanne, and Monet.

Bet Ooh, I like that one, and that one ...

Al Matisse, and Magritte.

Bet We walked for miles through the Louvre.

Al I like that one and that one.

Bet (*stopping*) I don't like that one.

Al And that one and that one.

Bet I don't like all that modern stuff, anybody could do it.

Al What, even me?

Bet You do do it, don't you?

Al I think we should go.

Bet Why?

Al Because we're never going to see it all, are we? So we might as well stop looking now.

Bet We've seen a lot, though.

Al We might as well stop looking now.

Bet All right, don't be so nasty.

Al The more we see, the more we don't know.

Bet Well, you know what you like n' that's all that matters.

Al Come on, let's get out.

Bet We can have another ten minutes, if you want ...

Al Ten minutes? You need ten years. Let's go.

Bet All right, keep your shirt on. We'll have another coffee.

Al Who's paying? We're going through the money, you know.

Bet I'll pay.

Al Is it my treat?

Bet Yeah.

Al Brilliant ... across from the Louvre, stop at a café and rest from an overdose of art. I mean, I'm just speechless.

Bet (*bringing him a chair*) The Parisians are a bit funny though, right off hand.

Al Well, it's their city, int it? They don't want louts like us messing it up.

Bet My feet are killing me. I'm gonna have to get a plaster ... And I want to take Rita's lad a T-shirt, there's some over there with Paris written on.

Al Well, what shall I do?

Bet Well, you sit here and wait.

Al Eh?

Bet You wait here and order me a cup of tea. And I fancy a bun, or sommat.

Al Eh?

Bet Yeah.

Al A bun.

Bet Or a cream cake. I could just eat a cream cake.

Al What, you mean stay here on me own, by myself?

Bet Yeah.

Al Oh, right.

Bet You'll be all right.

Al You'd better give me the book then.

Bet What for? You'll be all right — besides, I'm going to need the book, aren't I?

Al You're only going to get a T-shirt.

Bet I don't know what "plaster" is though, do I?

Al Well, what am I supposed to do?

Bet You'll be all right. Just say "tea". They'll know what you mean.

Al Oh, right.

Bet goes upstage. Al sits alone. He is extremely uncomfortable

So I sit, like a lemon on my own and wait outside the Café Rousseau.

Bet I'm looking at some T-shirts near the Louvre.

Al I hope she int going to be long.

Bet It's a change to be by myself, just looking, just wandering.

Al A waiter appears. (*He waves*) Eghhermp ... I'll let him go, get the next one.

Bet It's nice to be French for five minutes.

Al I play with an ash tray. Try and find it interesting.

Bet I try a bit of French — bonjour, je regardez. Eh, it works.

Al Beautiful café, int it? Across from here, I can see a water fountain, and through the water I just about make out the words Comédie Française. It certainly will be. I ignore everyone's nods and glances, I pretend I'm

not here, another waiter, I blank him, another, I cough, another, a
waitress, she's nice. She's coming straight for me, oh no ... oh no ... I
reach for a newspaper, pretend to read ... it's French. I can't read that ...
I'll leave it ... She's coming over, slowly coming over, her hair
cascading in the sunlight, slow motion, she comes to my table. I wish I
was dead ... I'm sat here smiling like a moron. Oh no ... Oh ... "bonjour,"
she says ... bonjour, what sort of bloody word is that, "bonjour"?

Bet Bonjour!

Al "Bonjour," she says.

Bet Bonjour!

Al Bonjour?

Bet Oh, it's great, int it?

Al She may as well talk to a stone ...

Bet Bonjour!

Al And I run for it.

Bet Merci, au revoir.

Al I make a dash while the waitress bonjours someone else, "Bonjour",
she says to an older woman who passes with one of them poodles. And
I'm up and away out of the danger zone ... (*He takes the chair UL and
walks quickly around the stage to Bet*) Oohhhhh, hang on.

Bet What are you doing?

Al Café was shut.

Bet It wasn't.

Al It was just closing, half-day apparently.

Bet Can't you do anything.

Al Nobody came, I'd been sat there an hour.

Bet Twenty minutes.

Al Nobody came.

Bet I can't leave you to do anything, can I?

Al Be fair, I'm playing away from home here.

Bet Yeah, I think I'll put you on the transfer list.

Al I waved but they all ignored me. You know what they say about the
French. I mean, they've got all this art and half of 'em are pig ignorant.

Bet And you're not.

Al I'd got it all worked out in my head. Je suis un croissant avec thè.

Bet I am a croissant with tea? Bloody hell. It's a good job you came away,
they might have thought you were an escaped lunatic.

Al Well, I can only just talk English, can't I ... I'm all right with French.

Bet To look ... je regardez. L'addition ... the bill. Je voudrais café noir ...
I would like a black coffee.

Al You're brilliant.

Bet You just have to try.

Al Have you just learnt that?

Bet Yeah.

Al You're brilliant, aren't you?

Bet Come on, let's go back to the hotel.

Al Where is it from here?

Bet Up this way ...

Al It's miles.

Bet We can get the Métro ...

Al I'm not getting the Métro.

Bet Why not?

Al I'm not getting the Métro, you get it if you want, I'm not arguing about it, but I'm not getting the Métro, no way. I don't like it.

Bet You've never been on it.

Al I don't like small spaces, I panic.

Bet Your shed's a small space.

Al It's not underground, is it?

Bet Hey, well, put your hand up if you want another cup of coffee.

Al (*putting his hand up*) Ool alla la ...

Bet Bon.

Al Très bon.

Bet Oui.

Al Oui, oui.

Bet Merci.

Al Bonjour.

Bet Bon voyage.

Al D'accord.

Bet Bloody hell ...

They move to the chairs, Bet UR, *Al* UL

Al Back at the hotel we change for our night in Paris ... massive room, int it? There's this massive bed, nearly as big as our house ...

Bet Don't exaggerate.

Al I'm not ...

Bet Have you had a bath?

Al Course I have ... and I've washed it after I've finished.

Bet There's a maid.

Al Is there?

Bet She'll come and pull the bed covers back. That fruit looked nice, didn't it?

Al I had an apple.

Bet And did you see them chocolates?

Al No.

Bet Yes, this morning there were two chocolates on the bed. I ate mine ...

Al I didn't have mine ...

Bet No, I had yours.

Al I don't know about you, but I'm tired out ... I could just go to bed.

Bet Ooo là là ...

Al Hey, you stop that ... It's like *It's a Knock Out*, all this chasing about.

Bet Are you ready? Let's get out there ...

Al I'll need a bloody holiday when we get back ...

Bet Right. Come on, let's hit the town.

Al Right. Pigalle, here we come ...

The Lights change to indicate Pigalle

Bet We're only going to look ...

Al Well, everybody does, don't they? Let's be honest ...

Bet We take a taxi ...

Al A taxi?

Bet As a treat, and we arrive at a Moulin Rouge thriving with bus trips, all of them wandering around Pigalle.

They use the audience as the sex supermarket

Al Seedy, int it?

Bet We pass a sex supermarket three times but we don't go in ...

Al We're not like that, are we ... You can't move for tourists up in Pigalle, and they're English, most of 'em.

Bet Don't you go out of my sight, I don't like it up here.

Al You'll be all rate wi' me.

Bet Oh ar ...

Al Nobody'll bother you while you're wi' me or they'll get a fat lip.

Bet It's weird up here ... sex shops all over ... weird ...

Al It's rate ...

Bet It's weird ... Eh, look at them pictures ...

Al It's rate, just keep hold of your handbag ...

Bet Do you want to hold it for me?

Al Not up here I don't.

Bet We couldn't afford the Folles.

Al Bloody rip off, sixty quid meal and show ...

Music plays quietly: "I Am What I Am" from La Cage aux Folles

They bring the chairs C *and sit. A spotlight picks them out*

Bet So we picked a club out of the blue and we've booked for an evening at Madame Arthur's, we don't know what it'll be like, but it's nice, clean inside, but it's dark and hot, like being in an oven, and it's sleazy but we like it, an' the waiters speak English. They bring us some wine ...

Al Well, here's to Paris ... cheers.

Bet Cheers.

Al And we sit and drink cheap red plonk.

Bet And he kisses me.

Al And food arrives and more wine.

Bet And I kiss him.

Al And we have oysters, prawns and snails.

Bet I left mine.

Al And then the lights went down. We didn't know what to expect, did we?

Bet And an hour later ...

Al The whole club is throbbing, clapping, I'm telling you I never thought I'd sit and watch grown blokes dressed up as women for three hours. It was brilliant, and we're laughing, aren't we? Laughing.

Bet I'm crying with laughing.

Al Everybody is ...

Bet And what's funny is their legs, they shave their legs.

Al She can't stop laughing at their legs, and they're in these awful tights, and the scenery shakes, and the music, the bloody music is awful, you can see the speakers shaking.

Bet And two wigs don't fit.

Al And one's got the wrong wig on ...

Bet But they keep coming out. Oh dear, funny.

Al And you love 'em.

Bet They charm you.

Al You love 'em. I never thought I'd sit through owt like that, but I'll tell you this, they worked bloody hard.

Pause. The music stops. Silence

Bet Wasn't it weird?

Al You look nice.

Bet What?

Al I said you look nice.

Bet Who?

Al You.

Bet I don't, my hair's all gone a mess.

Al You do ...

Bet You're drunk.

Al So what?

Bet So am I! How many bottles have we had?

Al I think I'll try and get another.

Bet Don't bother.

Pause

You look really nice, Al.

Al What?

Bet You look nice, attractive ...

Al No, no.

Bet What?

Al Say it again.

Bet What?

Al That other bit.

Bet What?

Al Say it again.

Bet (*giggling*) It again.

Al No.

Bet No.

Al No, just say what you said.

Bet I said I think you look nice, Al.

Al You never call me my name.

Bet I do.

Al You don't, you don't, you never call me my name.

Bet Don't I?

Al You never call me my name.

Bet I think I do.

Al I never call you your name.

Bet What is my name?

Al Dunno, I've forgot.

Bet You spoil everything, that could have been really nice and you spoil everything.

Al I don't, Bet ... I don't. See, I do know your name.

Bet You'll have forgotten it by the time you sober up, though.

They begin to move away from their seats. Al takes chairs R

Al That evening we stagger out of Madame Arthur's at half-past one in the morning ... and we're exhausted, aren't we? Absolutely tired out ... It'd be easier to go to the moon and back ...

Bet We're not going to walk, are we?

Al Are we hell, we'll get the Métro. Un carnet si'l vous plaît.

Bet Bloody hell. How did you know that?

Al I've been working it out all day.

Bet So we get on the Métro back to St Germain.

They stand C *with their arms in the air, holding the imaginary handles. Bet holds on to Al. The Lights change and they rock to simulate moving on the train*

Al Not bad is it?

Bet I'm not too keen this late at night. I don't like to be hemmed in.

Al Have you ever been on the Underground in London?

Bet I've never been to London.

Al What?

Bet No.

Al Don't look now but I think we're being watched.

Bet Where? (*She looks around*)

Al I said don't look.

Bet They might be pickpockets.

Al Might be.

Bet Do you think they know we're English?

Al I think they probably do, yeah.
Bet I've just seen 'em take that bloke's wallet.
Al Don't panic.
Bet What shall we do? They might have guns.
Al Don't panic.
Bet Do sommat, Al.
Al Hang on. They aren't bothering us, are they?
Bet They're still looking at us, though.
Al Just ignore 'em.
Bet They're looking at us. Look away from 'em.
Al You look away from 'em then.
Bet I am.
Al I said we should never have come on the Métro.
Bet They're coming over here.
Al Oh bloody hell.
Bet Look at 'em, they're like gypsies.
Al Don't look at 'em.
Bet They're coming, Al.
Al Just move this way.
Bet I can't move.
Al Watch your handbag.
Bet Where's the passports?
Al You've got mine.
Bet Do sommat.
Al What?
Bet Sommat.
Al Oh hell. You and them competitions. I could kill you.
Bet Do sommat.

Al suddenly breaks away from Bet and turns to the would-be muggers

Al (*screaming*) Arrrgh ... right, that's it. Come on then, come and get it
   if you want some of this you French bastards ... come on ... I'm English
   and I'm not having it. Come on all of you, I'll take you all on ... come
   on ... What are you looking at, come on, come on ... You stinking sods,
   I'll knock your bloody teeth out.
Bet Everyone on the Métro is looking at him.
Al Come on, you've picked the wrong 'un here ...
Bet The muggers get off the Métro and run up the platform.

Al Come on ...

Bet The whole of our carriage get off.

Al Look at 'em ...

Bet We are the only two people left on the Métro.

Al That did it.

Bet Scared half of Paris to bloody death. Are you OK?

Al I'm shaking like a leaf. Oh, my legs have gone, look at me shaking.

Bet I wonder if they were muggers.

Al Dunt matter, does it? If they were they've been chased off.

Bet And if they weren't?

Al Well, if they weren't there's four French blokes who think there's an English nutcase on the Métro ... Oh, I'm sweating with fear ...

Bet What would you have done, Al, if they'd've come for you?

Al Messed my pants, probably ...

The Lights change to indicate Notre Dame. Solemn organ music plays. It is the next morning and they have to prepare to leave Paris

Al exits and brings on their suitcases

Bet looks around. Al finds Bet lost in thought in Notre Dame

Al What are you playing at in here ... we're gunna miss the bus ...

Bet We can't go home without coming to Notre Dame, can we? Kneel down.

Al No, I'm not into that!

Bet Kneel down.

Al No.

Bet Come on.

Al I'd never do this at home.

Bet We're not at home.

Al Ohh.

Pause

Bet Just say a prayer.

Al I don't believe in owt.

Bet You can just say a prayer, can't you?

Al Yeah, I can do, I suppose.

Silence as they pray. Al attempts to attract Bet's attention

(*Finally*) What are you praying about?

Bet I'm not telling you.

Al Why not?

Bet Just say one. (*Pause*) Amen ... (*Pause*) Come on ... come on ... How long are you going to be?

Al I haven't finished yet. (*Pause*) Amen.

Bet You always have to overdo it, don't you?

Al I don't.

Bet What did you pray for?

Al That we didn't miss the boat.

Bet I just prayed for sommat nice ...

Al Who do you think was listening, Father Christmas?

Bet Don't make fun. What did you pray for?

Al I just wondered what it was all about, why we want to have everything. I just wondered why, if this is all there is, why aren't we nice to each other?

Bet Bloody hell.

Al It's just made me think, that's all.

Bet I thought that you didn't believe.

Al Well ...

Bet Well what?

Al Well, where's got to be sommat, ant there?

Bet I suppose so.

Al There's got to be sommat. I mean, we can't just be here alone, can we?

Bet You never know.

Al It'd be a bit frightening if we were just here on uz own. There's got to be sommat, hasn't there? Otherwise it is a sorry mess.

Bet Makes you think, doesn't it? There's so many good things in the world and I bet hardly anybody really sees 'em, we're lucky to be here, aren't we?

Al Very lucky, thanks to Bella.

Pause. They move R and sit

Do you wanna know what I've been thinking lately?

Bet No.

Al Shall I tell you?

Bet I don't know if I can take it.

Al Just lately I've been wondering what my life'll be like when you've
gone.

Bet What do you mean, "gone"? What do you mean, when I'm gone?

Al You know, gone, died. Passed on. I looked at that tomb and I imagined
I saw your name on it and I thought, God, my life'll be a mess whenever
Bet's not here.

Bet Oh, you're morbid.

Al That's what came into my head.

Bet Well, thanks a lot.

Al You wouldn't ever leave me, would you?

Bet Why should I stay with you?

Al Well, I love you.

Bet You never say it.

Al I've just said it.

Bet I could kill you sometimes, you know.

Al I know.

Bet No Al, I mean really kill you. Put a pillow over your face while you're
asleep, poison your coffee.

Al Don't say that in here ...

Bet I know, but I've thought about it. I've thought about killing you.

Al You haven't, you're only saying it.

Bet I'm not. I have thought about it — about what would happen, but I
never would.

Al Is that because you love me?

Bet No. I'm just scared of going to prison.

Pause

Al I don't want to go home. Do you?

Bet No.

Al There's nowt there. Let's stay here ... We could live like tramps, walk
around Paris, live off the land. I could get a job in Montmartre, painting.

Bet Go steady.

Al You don't think I'm any good, do you?

Bet Well, you're not, are you?

Pause

Al There's nowt to go back for. Stay here and slowly work our way across
     Europe, finish up in China or somewhere, then after a couple of years
     we could go back home. Wouldn't it be brilliant? No ties, just eating the
     world up, that'd be an education, wouldn't it?
Bet I've always fancied going to India.
Al Oooh, let's stay here, shall we? Let's bloody stay here!
Bet Ssshhh!

*Suddenly we hear Jacques Brel's "Ne Me Quitte Pas" loudly. The
atmosphere changes drastically. Paris is now a memory*

*Al brings on the floor of their box. Bet brings on the chairs. The two of
them carry on the back wall. The practical hanging light is visible
again*

   Al exits

Bet sits and listens

   Al enters. Pause. The music fades

Al Good tape, that. Glad we bought it.
Bet Yeah, good tape. I can't understand a bloody word of what he says.
     (*Pause*) Oh well.
Al Yeah.
Bet I wonder where it all went.
Al Ar.
Bet Shall I play it again?
Al No. We've been back a week and it's nearly worn out.

Pause

Bet Good laugh coming back, wasn't it?
Al Yeah.
Bet You did well, you only had one meal. And I wasn't sick. Good
     crossing, wasn't it? I could go on them North Sea Ferries all the time ...

Pause

Al Do you want a coffee?

Bet Oui ... I'll have et coffee au lait.
Al D'accord ... Je having café noir.
Bet Très bon. Avez vous una cuppa café noir?
Al Oui, oui.
Bet Bloody cold in here.
Al No, hang on ... I've got it. La chambre c'est fraise.

Pause

Bet The room is a strawberry? I think you should throw that phrase book
     away.
Al I just say owt, me ... Shall I put the heating on?

Pause

Bet You and that duty free.
Al Brilliant, int it?
Bet All that wine. And chocolates.
Al Brilliant.
Bet And cigs, you bought five hundred cigs. We don't even smoke.
Al I gave 'em to next door.
Bet Five hundred cigs?
Al Did you see me? I brought eight bottles of wine back.
Bet You daft sod ...
Al (*with a big sigh*) Oh dear ...
Bet Yeah.
Al I could eat sommat ...
Bet There's a plate of horse meat int kitchen.
Al Lovely.
Bet There's one of them croissants left if you want one.
Al Can do.
Bet (*with a sigh*) Shall we watch telly?
Al Ophhhhh ...
Bet We could watch a video.
Al A bloody video.
Bet We had a good time, didn't we? (*Pause*) Shall we play some records?
Al I'm going to my shed.

     Al exits

Bet (*to herself*) Oh dear ...

Al enters carrying a magazine. He is excited

Al Here's one ...
Bet What is it?
Al Here's one, I think we can do this one.
Bet OK, don't go manic, don't rush it.
Al Ha ha ... I think we can do this one.
Bet Go on ...
Al (*reading*) "Say in not more than fifteen words why you would like to go to Mexico."
Bet Mexico.
Al In not more than fifteen words.
Bet Mexico.
Al Go on then ...
Bet What?
Al Say sommat ...
Bet What's happened to that one about Euro Disney?
Al It's gone, it's int post. That wa' easy, I did that myself. How many times a year should you change your tooth brush, how many times a year should you brush your teeth.
Bet It was for kids ... Try and get sommat that rhymes, that always impresses 'em.
Al Here you are, what about this? "Mexico, Mexico, I wanna go, to Mexico."
Bet Why don't you leave it to me, let me do it?
Al All right then, know-all, here's one. "Mexico is a country full of spice, joy and culture with sand and sun and many a vulture."
Bet Do they have vultures in Mexico?
Al I don't know.
Bet You said that sun and sand bit about Florida.
Al I say the same in 'em all.
Bet And Greece.
Al It dunt matter ...
Bet You've got no patience with 'em.
Al "Mexico is a country that is spicy and hot ... and I want to go before I blow up ..."
Bet Listen, just listen to me for a minute.
Al What?

Bet You're doing 'em every ten minutes. It took me three weeks to do that one for Paris. Three weeks, sat looking through, working sommat out, and then it's the luck of the draw, it's a lottery ... I mean, how much have you spent on them magazines? You can't move in that shed for magazines. We could save that money and go to Whitby or somewhere.

Al What?

Bet We could have a run on a bus somewhere.

Al I'm not going to bloody Whitby.

Bet It'd be a break.

Al You go if you want, take Rita and Colin, they need a change of scenery.

Bet It's somewhere to go for a little break.

Al Bloody Whitby.

Bet You can see Dracula's tomb. Bram Stoker and that.

Al I'd rather hang myself.

Bet There's an Abbey.

Al I want to go somewhere, I don't want to go up the road, do I? We might as well buy a tent and camp int garden.

Bet Don't be daft, garden's not big enough.

Al I don't want to stop, I want to go somewhere.

Bet Oh, he's off.

Al Do you want to stop here ... look at it!

Bet I should have pushed you off that bloody boat.

Al Just bloody look at where we live!

Bet Go on, shout. Let's hear what a big man you are.

Al I'll call you sommat in a minute.

Bet Go on, little boy, you can't do a quiz so you're throwing a tantrum.

Al I said, didn't I? Once you've gone and had a look it's never the same. Once you've seen all that it's too much for your head.

Bet Why?

Al Because it's too bloody dangerous.

Bet Is it heck.

Al It is ... it is ...

Bet What's dangerous about it apart fom the Métro?

Al (*pointing to his head*) All this up here, because you go and see all that and then you come back, and it doesn't fit somehow, it's not big enough, there's no room. And just think, we've only seen that much (*he holds up his thumb and index finger*), we've only glanced at it ...

Bet At least we've been.

Al You come back and listen to everybody go on and on about us being a part of Europe — which part are we? They must think everybody's

bloody stupid here. We're not like them as far as I can see, we're a little
island, and them that's got gets on, and them that's not gets shit on ... and
it's going to get worse.

Bet There's probably people in France wi' no money, you know.

Al I'm not thick.

Bet We saw the best of it. I mean, there's probably people in France wi'
nowt.

Pause

Al Well, at least they've got nice bread.

Bet I bet some of 'em wished they lived here ...

Al I'll swap 'em.

Bet It's just different, int it?

Al We shouldn'ta been allowed to go to Paris, there ought to be a law
against it. It's too bloody dangerous, we might start getting ideas. We
might not want to watch *Catchphrase* or *Blind Date*.

Bet You don't watch 'em anyway.

Al We might start wanting sommat better.

Bet Allus in that bloody shed.

Al We might start wanting the pubs to open late, or cafés with good service
or decent wages or painters in the street, or buildings you can look at.
We might just start wanting sommat more ...

Bet We've got buildings.

Al What?

Bet We've got beautiful buildings.

Al Where ... where ... have we got owt decent?

Bet York.

Al Yeah, York, and that's it.

Bet Edinburgh.

Al You've never been.

Bet I saw it ont Holiday Programme. Bath. Marina's nice in Hull.

Al All right, I've heard you ...

Bet Beverley's nice, I think.

Al All right ... I get it.

Bet Bolton Abbey ... Castle Howard ... down by the bridge is nice on a
Sunday.

Al All right, I get the point.

Bet Aren't there any nice buildings in London?

Al It's all squashed up, int it, like everything here. You can't see it.

Bet France is bigger.
Al Thank you, Albert Einstein.
Bet (*musing*) Int it funny, you have to go abroad to see what we've got here, I think. I wouldn't mind going to Windsor Castle one day.
Al Windsor Castle? There's nowt there — it's all been burnt!
Bet Or on one of them "Whodunnit" weekends.
Al Whodunnit?
Bet There's nice buildings if you look. That's the trouble — we've never looked before, have we?
Al Bloody Whitby.
Bet Whitby'd be nice.
Al Whitby, who goes to Whitby?
Bet Or there's them Away Breaks. City break things. Gateshead. Seaburn.
Al Bloody Gateshead. Yipee! ... Bloody Metro Centre ...
Bet Captain Cook came from Whitby ... be sommat to look at, nice coast line.

Pause

Al (*sadly*) Bloody Seaburn.
Bet Have you finished in there?
Al More or less.
Bet Well, go and get it then, let's have a look.
Al No ... I'm not int mood.
Bet Go on, let's have a look at the new exhibition ...
Al (*slowly leaving*) Bloody Whitby, I could cry.

Al exits

Bet sits silently

Bet (*with a big sigh*) Oh dear ...

Al enters with a canvas, much more colourful than the first, with a montage of Parisian places on it. Al holds it so that Bet can't see it

Al Here you are ... turn around ... right. (*He holds up the painting*)
Bet Bloody hell, who's done that?
Al Him next door.
Bet It's brilliant.

Al S'all right, int it?
Bet I thought it was going to be another landscape.
Al So did I.
Bet We could sell that, get some cash.
Al I'm not selling it, it's taken me ages to do it.
Bet It's really good is that ... Why are them others so awful?

Pause

Al It's a different style, int it?
Bet It's Paris, int it?
Al It looks all right, dunt it?

Pause

Bet Mmmmm.
Al Anyway ...
Bet Yeah ...
Al Ah ...
Bet Yeah.
Al Shall I make a coffee?
Bet I'm not bothered.
Al No? (*Pause*) Yeah.
Bet Ohhhmmmm.

Pause

Al Arrrmmmm.

Pause

Bet Oh dear ...

Pause

Al "Hot as chilli, clear blue skies, Mexico is a big surprise."

Music plays: "La Bamba"

The Lights fade to Black-out

FURNITURE AND PROPERTY LIST

ACT I

On stage: 2 white chairs

Off stage: Copy of *Bella*
Canvas with monochromatic industrial landscape (**A1**)
Letter (**Det**)
Lifebuoy (**A1**)
2 suitcases (**A1** and **Bet**)
Tourist guide (**A1**)
2 windjammers (**Bet**)

ACT II

Strike: 2 white chairs

On stage: 2 Parisian chairs

Off stage: 2 white chairs (**Bet**)
Magazine (**A1**)
Canvas with montage of Parisian places (**A1**)
2 suitcases (**A1**)

LIGHTING PLOT

Practical fitting required: hanging light

ACT I
To open: Full general lighting

Cue 1	**Intro music plays** *Fade house lights*	(Page 1)
Cue 2	**Bet** sits and reads *Dim lights*	(Page 1)
Cue 3	**Bet:** "You shuddup." *Black-out, then immediately bring up lights*	(Page 7)
Cue 4	**Bet:** " ... to show for it except you." *Black-out, then immediately bring up lights*	(Page 10)
Cue 5	**Bet:** "I'll go with Rita." *Black-out*	(Page 12)
Cue 6	**Music plays: "Vesoul"** *Bring up lights*	(Page 12)
Cue 7	**Bet** dances on with her suitcase *Spot on* **Bet**	(Page 12)
Cue 8	**Bet** picks up her case *Turn off spot*	(Page 13)
Cue 9	**Al:** " ... have a dance will you?" *Disco lights* DL; *spot on* **Al**	(Page 21)
Cue 10	**Bet:** " ... I'm boiling." *Lights change to blue with cloud effect*	(Page 22)
Cue 11	**Music plays: "Les Bourgeois"** *Fade to Black-out*	(Page 28)

ACT II

To open: Full general lighting

Cue 12 **Bet:** " ... how women can resist you." (Page 35)
      Lights change to Louvre effect; power white light
        for Mona Lisa effect

Cue 13 **Al:** "Pigalle, here we come ..." (Page 40)
      Lights change to Pigalle effect

Cue 14 **Bet** and **Al** sit c (Page 41)
      Spot on **Bet** *and* **Al**

Cue 15 **Bet** and **Al** stand c with arms in the air (Page 43)
      Lights change to Métro effect

Cue 16 **Al:** "Messed my pants, probably ..." (Page 45)
      Lights change to Notre-Dame effect

Cue 17 Music: "La Bamba" (Page 54)
      Lights fade to Black-out

EFFECTS PLOT

ACT I

ACT II